# First World War
## and Army of Occupation
# War Diary
## France, Belgium and Germany

50 DIVISION
150 Infantry Brigade,
Brigade Trench Mortar Battery
11 April 1916 - 31 August 1916

WO95/2837/4

The Naval & Military Press Ltd
www.nmarchive.com
**Published in association with The National Archives**

Published by

## The Naval & Military Press Ltd

Unit 10 Ridgewood Industrial Park,

Uckfield, East Sussex,

TN22 5QE England

Tel: +44 (0) 1825 749494

www.naval-military-press.com

www.nmarchive.com

*This diary has been reprinted in facsimile from the original. Any imperfections are inevitably reproduced and the quality may fall short of modern type and cartographic standards.*

© **Crown Copyright**
**Images reproduced by permission of The National Archives, London, England, 2015.**

# Contents

| Document type | Place/Title | Date From | Date To |
|---|---|---|---|
| Heading | WO95/2837 50 Div 150 Inf Bde Bde Trench Mortars Apr 16-Aug 16 | | |
| Heading | 50 Div 150 Bde Trench Mortar Bty To 1916 Apr To 1916 Aug | | |
| War Diary | Sheet 28 N.29.d.7.9 | 11/04/1916 | 26/04/1916 |
| War Diary | Sheet 27 Q.35.b.3.4 | 27/04/1916 | 30/04/1916 |
| War Diary | Sheet 28 N.29.d.7.9 | 11/04/1916 | 26/04/1916 |
| War Diary | Sheet 27 Q.35.b.3.4 | 27/04/1916 | 30/04/1916 |
| Heading | War Diary Vol I 150th T.M. Battery May 1916 | | |
| War Diary | Field | 01/05/1916 | 31/05/1916 |
| Heading | War Diary Vol II 150 T.M Battery June 1916 | | |
| War Diary | Field | 01/06/1916 | 30/06/1916 |
| Heading | War Diary 150th Trench Mortar Battery July 1916 Volume X | | |
| Miscellaneous | Attached In War Diary For Month Of July | 01/08/1916 | 01/08/1916 |
| War Diary | Kemmel Map Sheet 28 | 01/07/1916 | 31/07/1916 |
| War Diary | Kemmel | 01/08/1916 | 31/08/1916 |

WO95/2837 (4)

50 Div    150 INF BDE

BDE TRENCH MORTARS

Apr'16 – Aug'16

~~ARMY TROOPS~~

50 DIV
150 BDE.

### 150
TRENCH MORTAR BTY

1916 APR TO 1916 AUG

(2693)

Army Form C. 2118.

# WAR DIARY
or
## INTELLIGENCE SUMMARY.
*(Erase heading not required.)*

1/50/1 French Motor Factory

Instructions regarding War Diaries and Intelligence Summaries are contained in F. S. Regs., Part II. and the Staff Manual respectively. Title pages will be prepared in manuscript.

| Place | Date | Hour | Summary of Events and Information | Remarks and references to Appendices |
|---|---|---|---|---|
| Sheet 2.B. M 29 c 2.9 | 11.4.16 | | Detachment under Lt Ebro arrived at Veaves at 9pm stay the night on | |
| | 12.4.16 | | IV 29. 6. 1.9 | |
| | | | Next arrived from Chocolaterie & arranged dug out. Some I am. woodwork brought | |
| | | | up. No food seen. Nothing shot down owing to heavy rain. | |
| | 13.4.16 | | Found positions for guns. | |
| | 14.4.16 | | Commenced emplacements En. & N.A. | |
| | 15.4.16 | | Continued work on emplacements | |
| | 16.4.16 | | Continued work on emplacements in E.H. & continued bomb store in N.A. | |
| | 17.4.16 | 9am | 2 cars 3 mounts from gun in E.2 brought in | |
| | | | Reliefs Lt McRae, 1 N.C.O. & 5 men moved here. Lt Silver, 1 N.C.O. & 5 men | |
| | | | said to do from gun in G.H. no attention to enemy aeroplanes owing to adverse | |
| | | | weather rendering W.T. work would be done | |
| | | | Very rainy. On the evening a shell if 15cm burst in [?] left of Boche sector. | |
| | | | the gun in G.H. was ordered to produce on the support trench G.3. 30 rounds | |
| | | | Ver E.2 was called upon for retaliation & fired 3 rounds on [?] | |
| | 18.4.16 | 11am | no smell be seen fell on the enemy front line trench In the evening | |

Army Form C. 2118.

# WAR DIARY
## or
## INTELLIGENCE SUMMARY.
(Erase heading not required.)

Instructions regarding War Diaries and Intelligence Summaries are contained in F. S. Regs., Part II. and the Staff Manual respectively. Title pages will be prepared in manuscript.

| Place | Date | Hour | Summary of Events and Information | Remarks and references to Appendices |
|---|---|---|---|---|
| | 19.4.16 | | Hype Riley gun was killed by a stray bullet whilst catching something to a dug out. Raining again. In retaliation to enemy rifle grenades, fired 19 rounds from the gun in F2. There were 4 failures. The enemy was otherwise very busy on the right front. Cpl Dixon came up to cup love casualty. | |
| | 20.4.16 | | Weather somewhat better. | |
| | | 11am | Again put a stop to enemy from rifle grenades by 10 rounds from gun in F2. Men in right Batt Sector relieved. Stood to in the evening in accordance with instructions from the Infantry. | |
| | 21.4.16 | | Weather fine. Early the afternoon turned to rain. The enemy are very active on our left + the staff gradually worked round the more direct from 6 and broken fire gun in F2 + taken another 6 rounds in reply to enemy undetermined. Ple Keyse went sick | |
| | 22.4.16 | | Weather not nothing doing | |
| | 23.4.16 | | Fine. Quiet except for a large quantity aeroplanes | |
| | 24.4.16 | | Ple Agar wounded in wrist. D Hunt Kitson received a bad rocken at 17pm. | |
| | 25.4.16 | | Compelled took stone in H1A. Quiet day | |
| | 26.4.16 | | Quiet day. Stood to practically all night. | |

T2134. Wt. W708—776. 500000. 4/15. Sfr J. C. & S.

Army Form C. 2118.

# WAR DIARY
## or
## INTELLIGENCE SUMMARY.
(Erase heading not required.)

Instructions regarding War Diaries and Intelligence Summaries are contained in F. S. Regs., Part II. and the Staff Manual respectively. Title pages will be prepared in manuscript.

| Place | Date | Hour | Summary of Events and Information | Remarks and references to Appendices |
|---|---|---|---|---|
| Abeele | 27.4.16 | | Relieved by 76/1 Trench Mortar Battery. All guns brought out of the line | |
| Q.35 & 3.4 | 28.4.16 | | Marched to rest billets | |
| | 29.4.16 | | Fatigues | |
| | 30.4.16 | | Rest | |

Quenton Kirkwood Lieut
O.C. 150/1 Trench Mortar Battery.

Duplicate

Army Form C. 2118.

150/1 TM/15/4

# WAR DIARY
or
INTELLIGENCE SUMMARY

(Erase heading not required.)

Instructions regarding War Diaries and Intelligence Summaries are contained in F.S. Regs., Part II. and the Staff Manual respectively. Title Pages will be prepared in manuscript.

| Place | Date | Hour | Summary of Events and Information | Remarks and references to Appendices |
|---|---|---|---|---|
| About 2.2 N.29 d 7.9 | 11-4-16 | | Detachment under 2/Lieut Culzean arrived at Harrison at 7pm. Stayed night at N.29 c.1-9 | |
| | 12-4-16 | | Went round front line trenches & arranged dug outs. Lewis & ammunition brought up to front line. Nothing else doing. Rain & heavy snow. Found positions for guns. | |
| | 13-4-16 | | Commenced emplacements in F1 & H1A | |
| | 14-4-16 | | Continued work on emplacements | |
| | 15-4-16 | | Continued work on emplacements in F1 & H1A | |
| | 16-4-16 | | Fired 3 rounds from gun in F2 to register | |
| | 17-4-16 | 9am | Relief. 2/Lt Woolner & 1 NCO & 5 men arrived to relieve 2/Lt Culzean, 1 NCO & 5 men | |
| | | noon | Fired 6 rounds from gun in G.H in retaliation for enemy sausages. Enemy to adverse machine gun. Bills might could be drawn. | |
| | 18-4-16 | | Very heavy. On the afternoon and at noon 2/Lt Sherwin on exploring left of Battalion line the gun in G.H was ordered to open fire in the support trench at G.5. The gun in F2 was called upon for retaliation & fired 3 rounds. All 9 struck on the enemy parapet. As was fell in the enemy front line trench. In the evening 2/Lt Sherwin was killed by a stray bullet while adding rounds to string out. | |
| | 19-4-16 | 11am | Raining again. In retaliation to enemy rifle grenades fired 14 rounds from gun in F2. This was effective. The enemy was otherwise very quiet. | |

Army Form C. 2118.

# WAR DIARY
## or
## INTELLIGENCE SUMMARY

*(Erase heading not required.)*

Duplicate

Instructions regarding War Diaries and Intelligence Summaries are contained in F. S. Regs., Part II. and the Staff Manual respectively. Title Pages will be prepared in manuscript.

| Place | Date | Hour | Summary of Events and Information | Remarks and references to Appendices |
|---|---|---|---|---|
| | 21.4.16 | | on the whole front. Cpl Dixon came up to replace casualty. Weather somewhat better. | |
| | | 11 am | Again put a stop to enemy rifle grenades by 10 rounds from gun in F2. Burst on Right Om richer observed. Stood to in the morning in the manner usual down from the infantry | |
| | 22.4.16 | | Weather fine but in the afternoon turned to rain. The enemy were very active in our left & the whole 7 Dichards worked normal this way. About 3pm fired 15 rounds from gun in F3 & later another 10 rounds in reply to enemy machine gun. Weapons not used | |
| | 22.4.16 | | Nothing much - nothing doing | |
| | 23.4.16 | | Fine. Quiet except for a large quantity of minnenwerfers. | |
| | 24.4.16 | | Pte Agans wounded in hip. Direct citizen received & heat nearlies at 5pm | |
| | 25.4.16 | | Compared bomb gun in H1A. Quiet day. | |
| | 26.4.16 | | Quiet day. Fired 15 practically all night | |

Army Form C. 2118.

Duplicate.

# WAR DIARY
## or
## INTELLIGENCE SUMMARY
*(Erase heading not required.)*

Instructions regarding War Diaries and Intelligence Summaries are contained in F. S. Regs., Part II. and the Staff Manual respectively. Title Pages will be prepared in manuscript.

| Place | Date | Hour | Summary of Events and Information | Remarks and references to Appendices |
|---|---|---|---|---|
| Sheet 27 Q 35. b 3.4 | 27.4.16 | | Relieved by 76/1 Trench Mortar Battery. All guns brought out of the line. | |
| | 28.4.16 | | Marched to rest billets | |
| | 29.4.16 | | Fatigues | |
| | 30.4.16 | | Rest | |

Denman Lieutenant
O.C. 150/1 Trench Mortar Battery.

# War Diary

## Vol I

## 150th T.M. Battery

## May 1916

A.W. Atkinson Capt.
OC 150th TMB

Army Form C. 2118.

# WAR DIARY
## or
## INTELLIGENCE SUMMARY

VOLUME I ~~VolI~~

(Erase heading not required.)

Instructions regarding War Diaries and Intelligence Summaries are contained in F. S. Regs., Part II. and the Staff Manual respectively. Title Pages will be prepared in manuscript.

| Place | Date 1916 | Hour | Summary of Events and Information | Remarks and references to Appendices |
|---|---|---|---|---|
| Field | May 1st-25th | | The Battery was at Ennestorik. Warning: Two reserve sections were formed. One from 4th & 5th Yorks and one from 4th Yorks Regt. That two sections were formed into the 150/2 Battery. | |
| | 26th | | 150/2 Battery was established under command of 2nd Lieut £B Warter of 5th Yorks Regt. | |
| | 26th | 10pm | Batteries 150/1 & 150/2 returned to Kemmel and took over trenches E1-H1 a inclusive from 96" Trench. 150/1 took over new E1-F5 incl. & 150/2 G1-H1a incls. | |
| | 27th | | Guns were regulated from all emplacements and a supply of Ammunition taken up. | |
| | 28th | 3-5pm | 2 Guns in 150/2 Left fired 200 rounds on enemy front line in retaliation for sausages. | |
| | 29th | 10pm | Emplacement was commenced on right of Broadway behind G4. | |
| | 30th | 4pm | Guns behind E3 fired 100 rounds in retaliation for light sausage minniers. | |
| | 31st | 3.30pm | Emplacement behind E3 was slightly damaged by a minnie was repaired overnight. | |

Averdwoon Capt.
OC 150th Trench

2449  Wt. W14957/Mgo  750,000  1/16  J.B.C. & A.  Forms/C.2118/12.

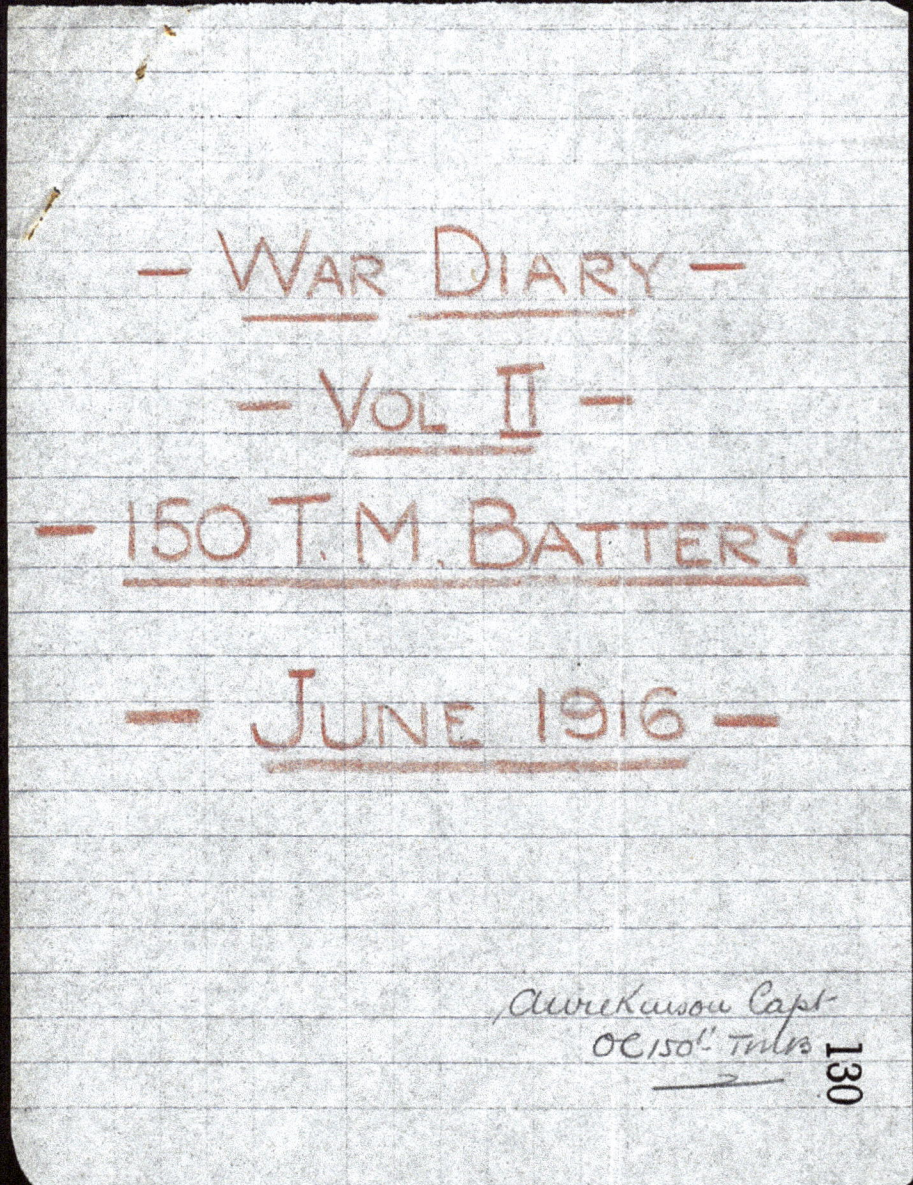

# War Diary
## Vol II
### 150 T.M. Battery
#### June 1916

A. McKinson Capt.
O.C. 150th T.M.B.

Army Form C. 2118.

# WAR DIARY
## or
## INTELLIGENCE SUMMARY
### VOLUME II

Vol III

(Erase heading not required.)

Instructions regarding War Diaries and Intelligence Summaries are contained in F.S. Regs., Part II. and the Staff Manual respectively. Title Pages will be prepared in manuscript.

| Place | Date June. | Hour | Summary of Events and Information | Remarks and references to Appendices |
|---|---|---|---|---|
| Field | 1st | | | |
| | 2nd | 4pm | A large Amm Store was commenced in G3 support trench | |
| | | | Guns in F5 and G1 fired 50 rounds each on trenches opposite in relation for sausages | |
| | 3rd | | Store in G3 was emptied and filled with Ammunition. | |
| | 4th | | Large Store started in the Gully just in front of SP11. | |
| | 5th | 3/1 am | Gun position in G1 blown in by trifine, and one in the trench badly damaged by 5.9 Shell. | |
| | 6th | | Position in the trench reconstructed and strengthened. | |
| | 7th/18th | | About 1000 rds fired in relation mostly between the hours of 2 & 5 p.m. for sausages and exit tips etc. A new position was built in G1 and one three temporary positions were made in G2 & G3 support. | |
| | 19th | 10 pm | Handed over trenches to 73 Tr'M. battery. | |
| | 20th | | Proceeded to Wittounie | |
| | 21st | | Proceeded to St Jean Cappell | |
| | 22nd | | At St Jean Cappell. | |
| | 23rd | | Returned to Kemmel Shelters to prepare for 4th East Yorks & 4th Yorks raid. | |
| | 24th | | Prepared gun ammunition & emplacements for raids | |
| | 25th | | Sections went into trenches F5 & G3 & registered guns on raiding points. | |
| | 26th | 12 midnight -2 am | Barrage was formed on flanks of raiding parties. 600 rds were fired until Bde returned trenches. | |
| | 27th to 31st | | Battery left the trenches in the early morning & proceeded to Bethune where it rested. | |

Aurkinson Capt.
OC 170th TM B3

2449 Wt. W14957/M90 750,000 1/16 J.B.C. & A. Forms/C.2118/12.

War Diary

150th Trench Mortar Battery

July 1916

Volume +.

Coy. Hd: Qrs.
    150th Inf: Bde.

    Attached is War Diary for month of July.

                              A Wilkinson Capt
                                O.C. 150th T.M.B.

1.8.16.

**Army Form C. 2118.**

# WAR DIARY
## or
## INTELLIGENCE SUMMARY
*(Erase heading not required.)*

Instructions regarding War Diaries and Intelligence Summaries are contained in F. S. Regs., Part II. and the Staff Manual respectively. Title Pages will be prepared in manuscript.

| Place | Date | Hour | Summary of Events and Information | Remarks and references to Appendices |
|---|---|---|---|---|
| KEMMEL | 1. | — | Battery at rest at Berken. | |
| MAP SHEET 28 | 2. | 10pm | Took over from 149 A Bde. Trenches H2-L5 inclusive. | |
| | 3. | 9 am. | Registered all positions. | |
| | 4. | 11 am. | Fired 25 rounds from Trench K1 in retaliation. | |
| | 5. | — | Worked on positions in K & L Trenches. | |
| | 6. | — | Fresh amm. & replenished all stores. | |
| | 7. | 2 pm. | Fired 40 rounds on wire & crater from K1. | |
| | 8. | 9 pm. | Commenced new position in J4. Also made temporary position in front of L15. Took over trenches G1-H11 incl. from 73 Bde. | |
| | 9. | — | Finished position in J4. Registered Gun for pairs & got amm: dugs to store. | |
| | 10. | 1 am. | Stood to during raid on craters but no firing done. | |
| | 11. | 10 pm. | Moved amm: Stock from L15 temporary position. | |
| | 12. | 3 pm. | 43 rounds fired into Petit Bois from K1 in retaliation for sausages. | |
| | 13. | 9 pm. | Worked on new position behind L5. | |
| | 14. | 2.30 pm. | 90 rounds fired on craters Petit Bois from K1. 56 rounds on Craters from J2. | |
| | 15. | 3.30 pm. | New position behind L5 blown in by mine. | |
| | 16. | — | Cleaning amm: & carrying from L5 position. | |
| | 17. | 4.30 pm | One man wounded by pistol light grenade in L1. | |
| | 18. | — | | |
| | 19. | 3 pm. | 10 Rds fired from L1 & 10 from K1 in retaliation. | |
| | 20. | 1 am. | 1 Officer & 1 man killed. 1 NCO & 5 men wounded. All in SP3 now by digg. Tunng. | |
| | 21. | — | | |
| | 22. | — | Strengthening Dugouts in SP11. | |
| | 23. | 9 pm. | 151st Bde took over trenches G1-G4 incl. | |
| | 24. | — | Defensive position started in Washing Street. 10 rds fired on Hammer Head from H1a. | |
| | 25. | — | Work done on new position in Washing Street. | |
| | 26. | — | New position started in L6. Gun registered from Washing Street. Fired over J2 & L2. | |
| | 27. | — | New position started in J10. | |
| | 28. | — | } Work done on new positions | |
| | 29. | — | | |
| | 30. | — | New defensive position near SP13 old commenced. | |
| | 31. | — | Work done on all new positions. | |

Atwickinson Capt.
OC. 150th TMB.

# 150TH TM BATTERY.
## WAR DIARY or INTELLIGENCE SUMMARY

**Army Form C.**
**VOLUME IV**
**AUGUST 1916**

| Place | Date Aug/16 | Hour | Summary of Events and Information |
|---|---|---|---|
| Rummel | 1. | | No firing done. Work done on emplacements in L6 and leading sheet. |
| | 2. | | Work done on the three new emplacements with L6. No leading sheet. |
| | 3. | | Guns reported from the three new emplacements on Enemy lines. |
| | 4. | 4pm | 50 Rounds fired from T.6 on to trench in front of Petit Bois. |
| | 5. | | Ammunition cleaned and stored at new emplacements. |
| | 6. | 3am | About 20 rounds fired on Petit Bois in retaliation from L2. |
| | 7. | | Handed over to 56½ T.M Battery. |
| | 8. | | Moved to Thieushouk & stayed until the 10th. |
| | 11. | | Entrained to Doullens - marched to Authieux. Stayed at Authieux until 12.11.14. |
| | 15. | | Marched to Heavelles - remained one night. |
| | 16. | | Marched to Molleur aux Bois - stayed one night. |
| | 17. | | Marched to Millencourt. |
| | 18-31 | | Stayed at Millencourt and carried on training, taking part in bow being attacks on the 25th & 26th. Also in Brigade attacks on the 27th & 30th & 31st. 10 men per battalion were trained for firing stokes Ammunition. 10 men per battalion were also trained in the use of stokes guns, with exception of firing. |

Authinson Capt
O. 150th TMB

www.ingramcontent.com/pod-product-compliance
Lightning Source LLC
Chambersburg PA
CBHW081510160426
43193CB00014B/2640